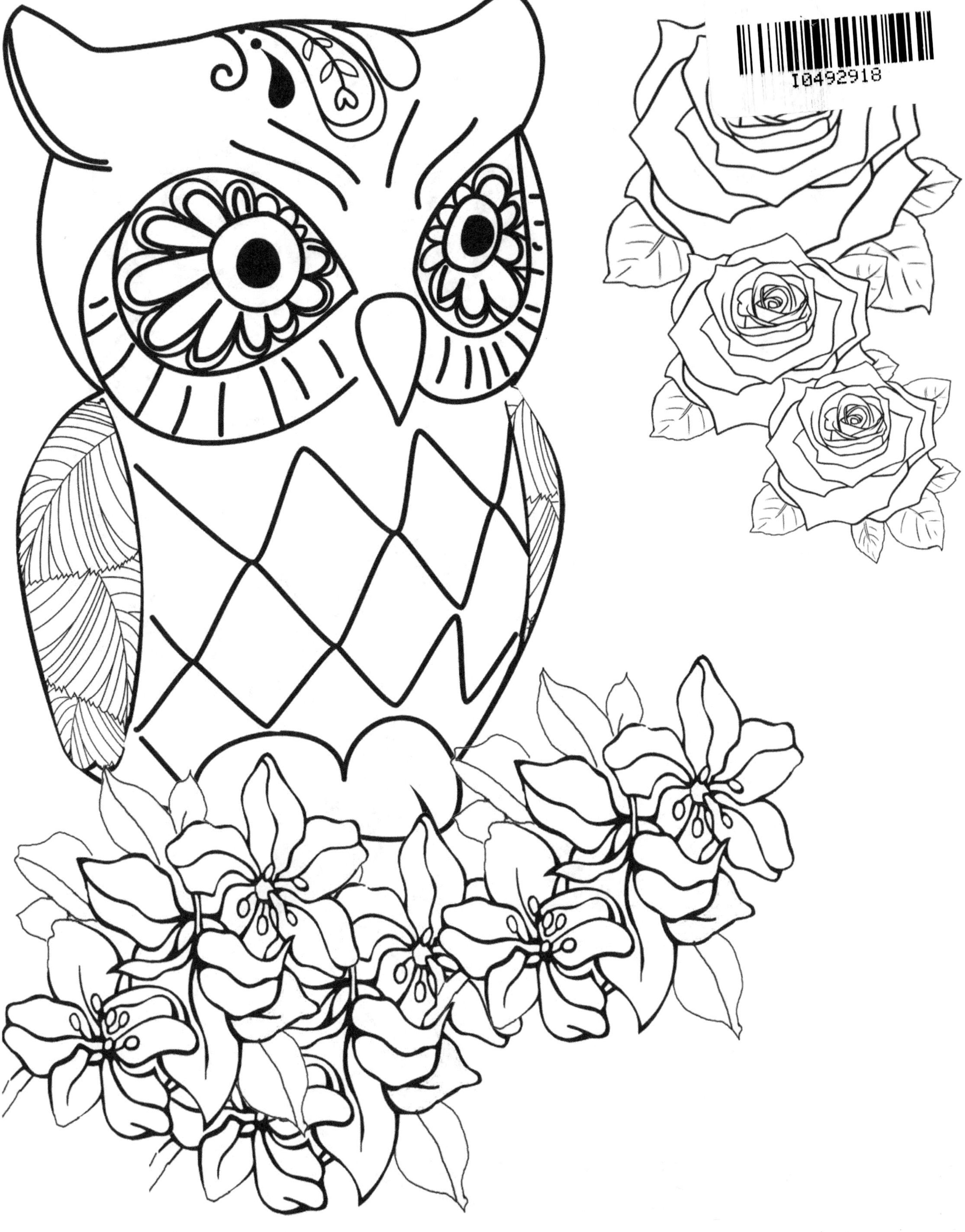

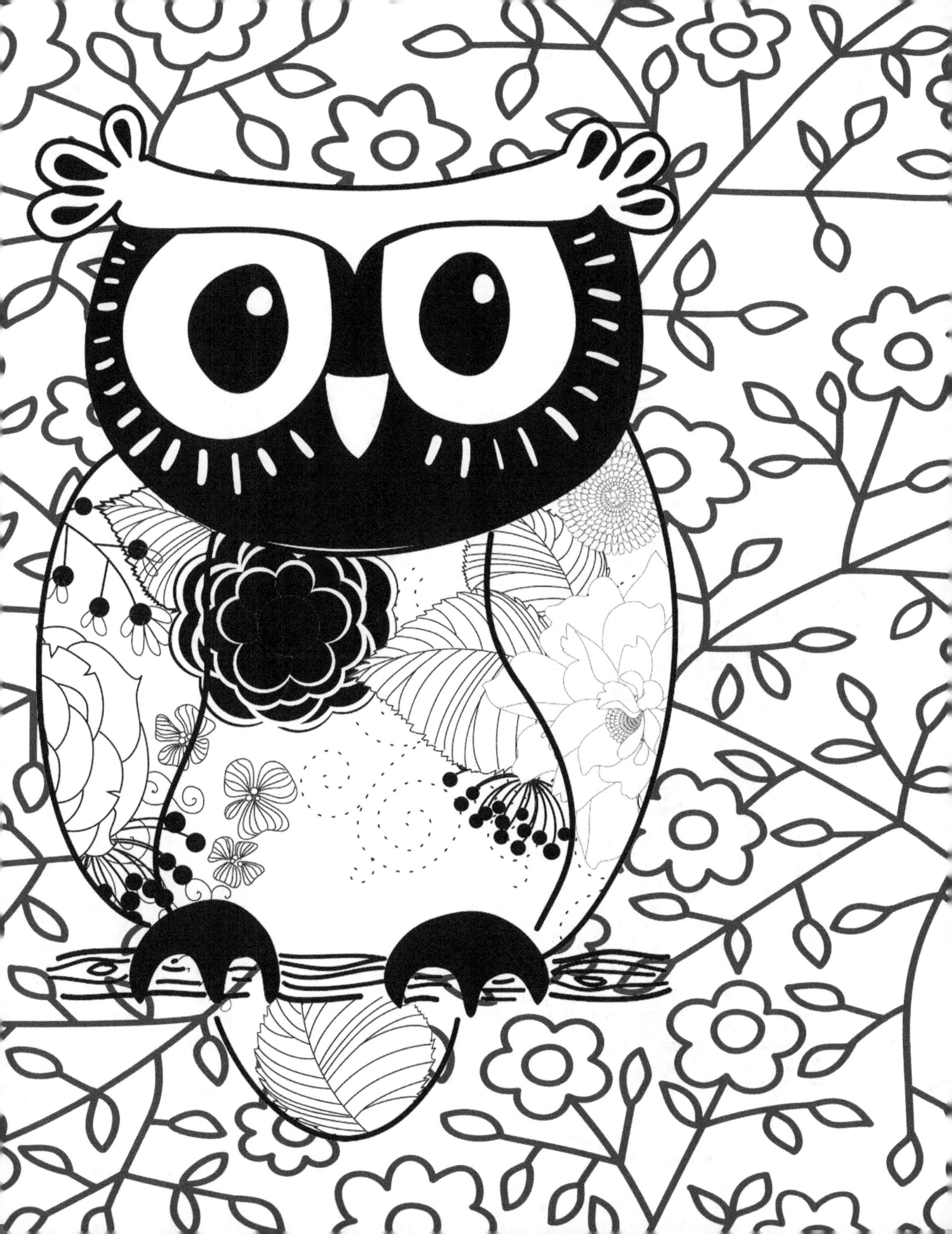

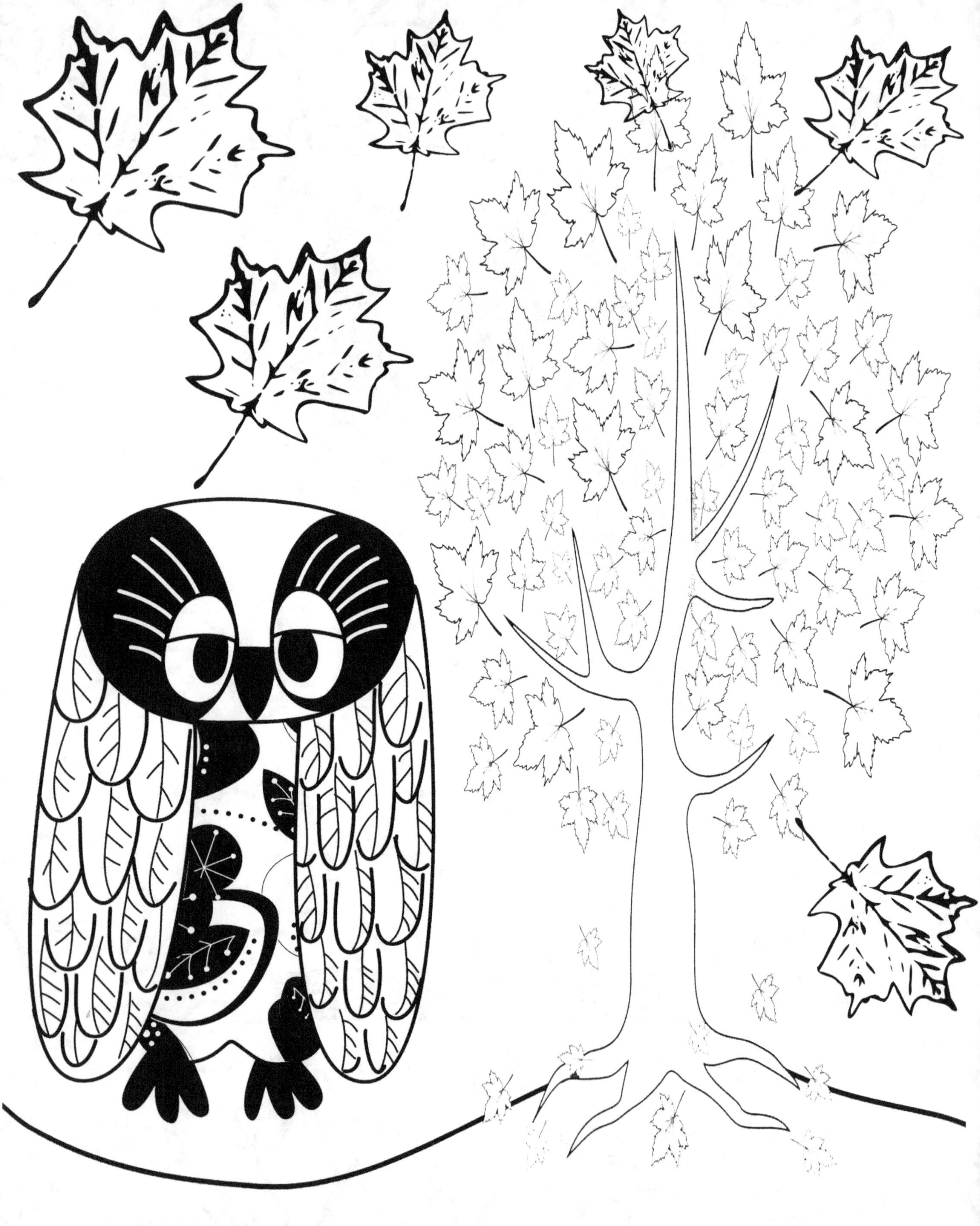

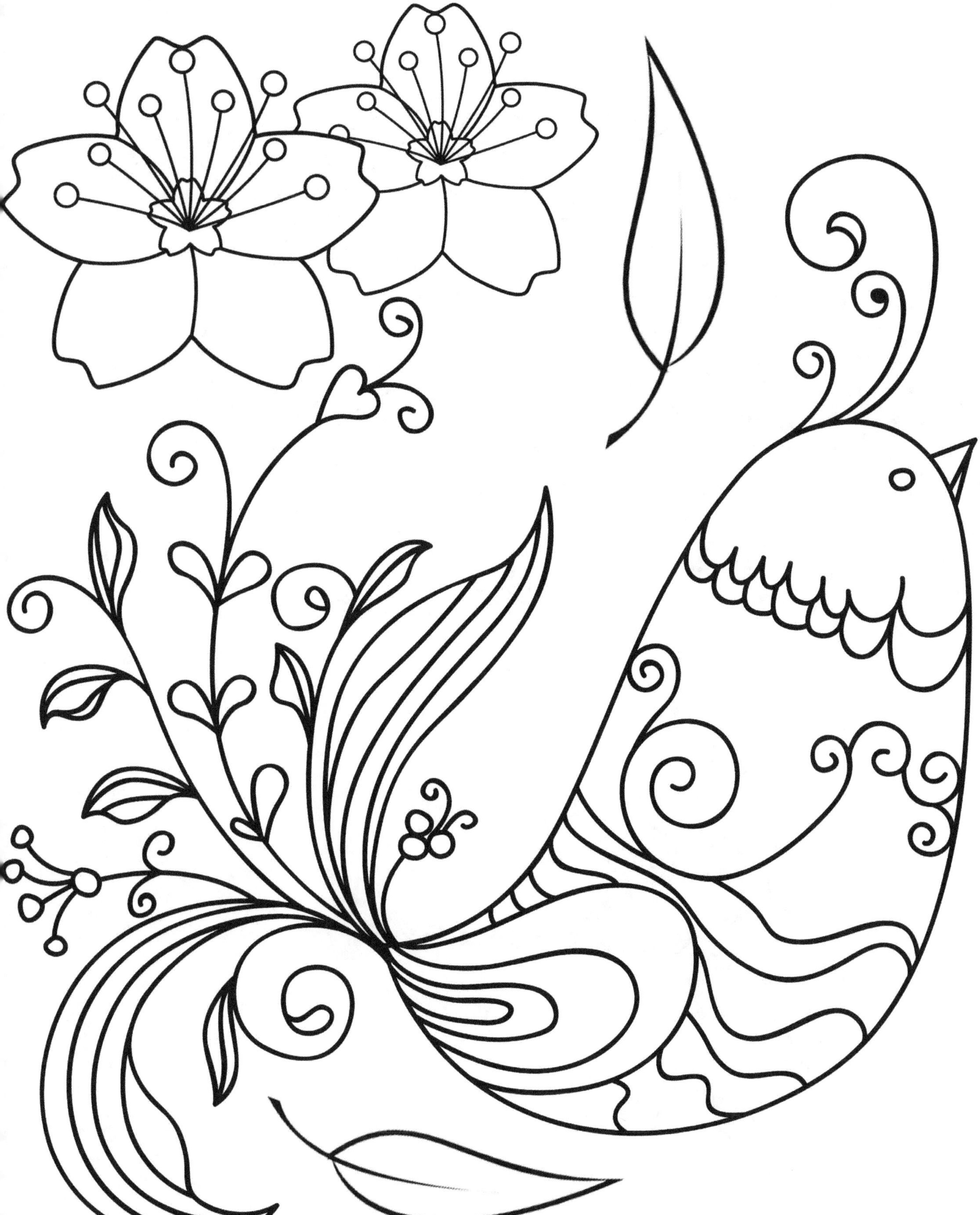

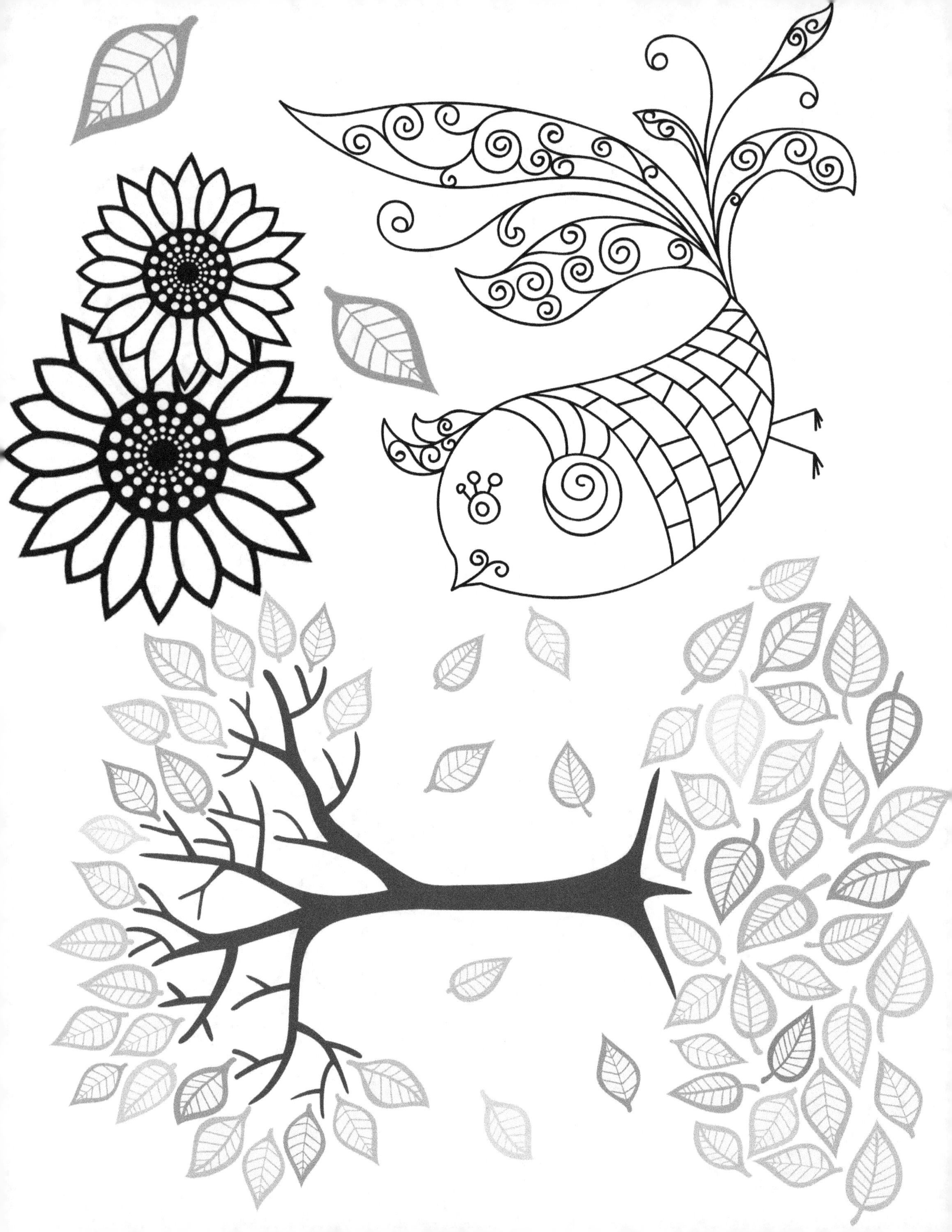

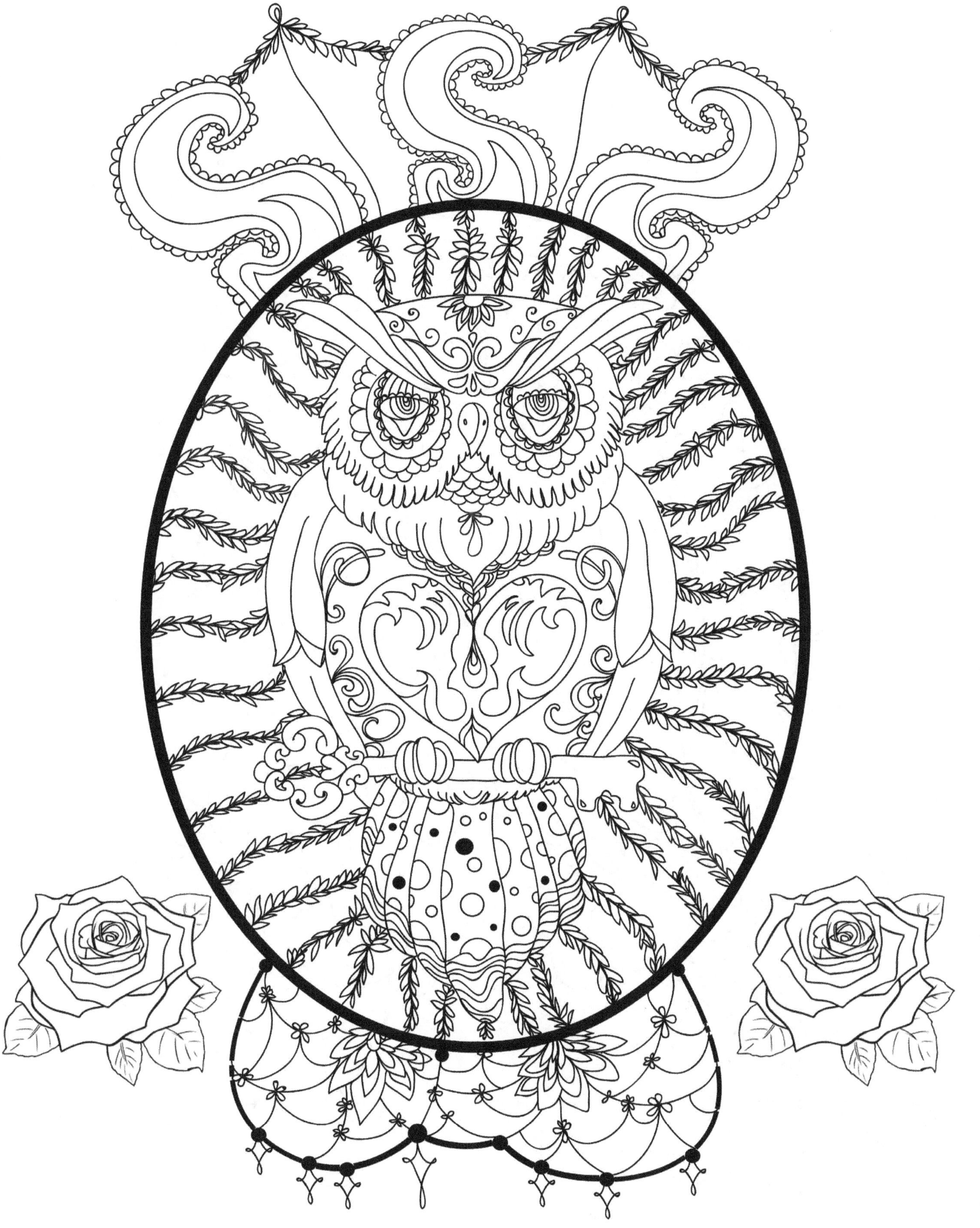

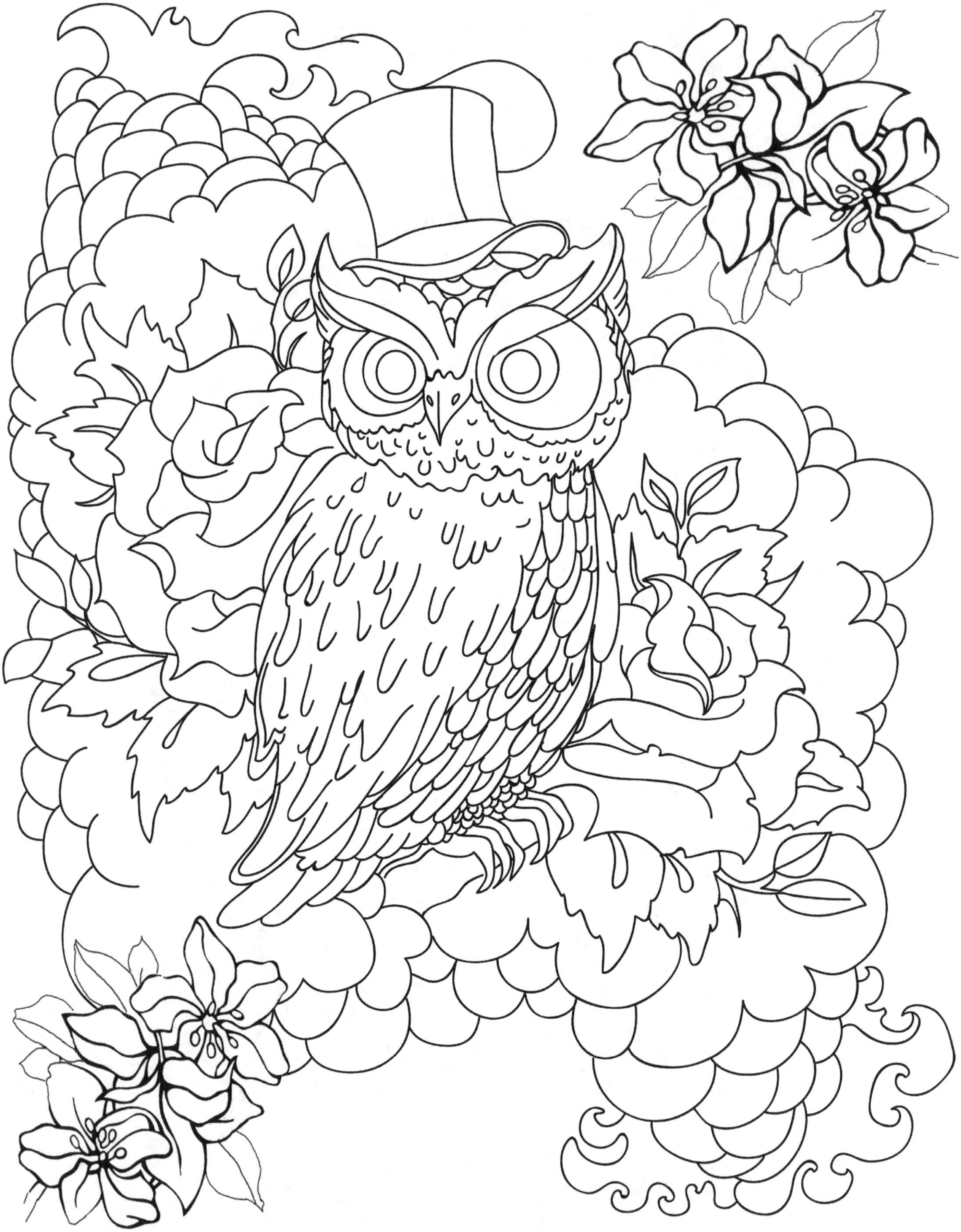

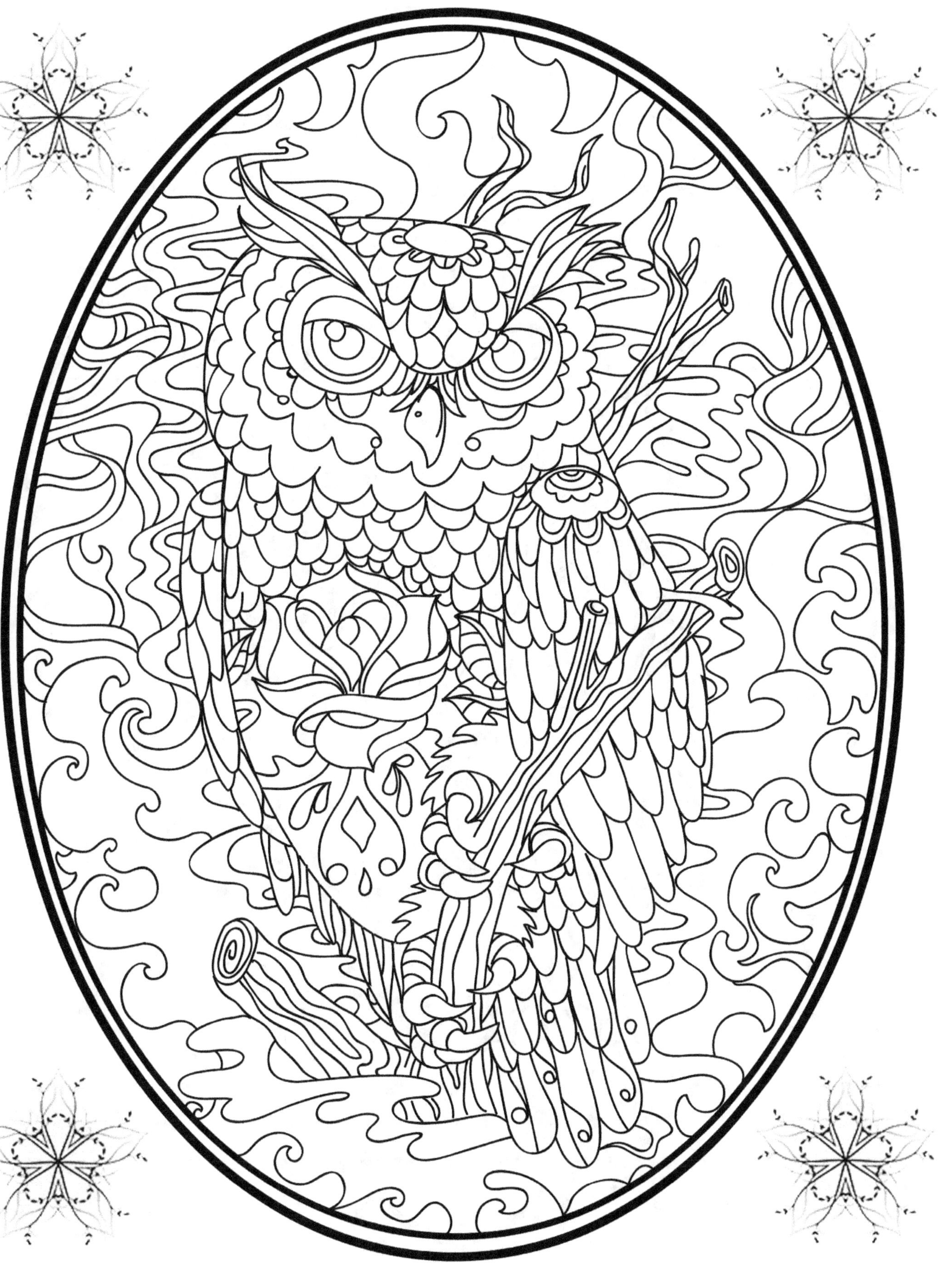

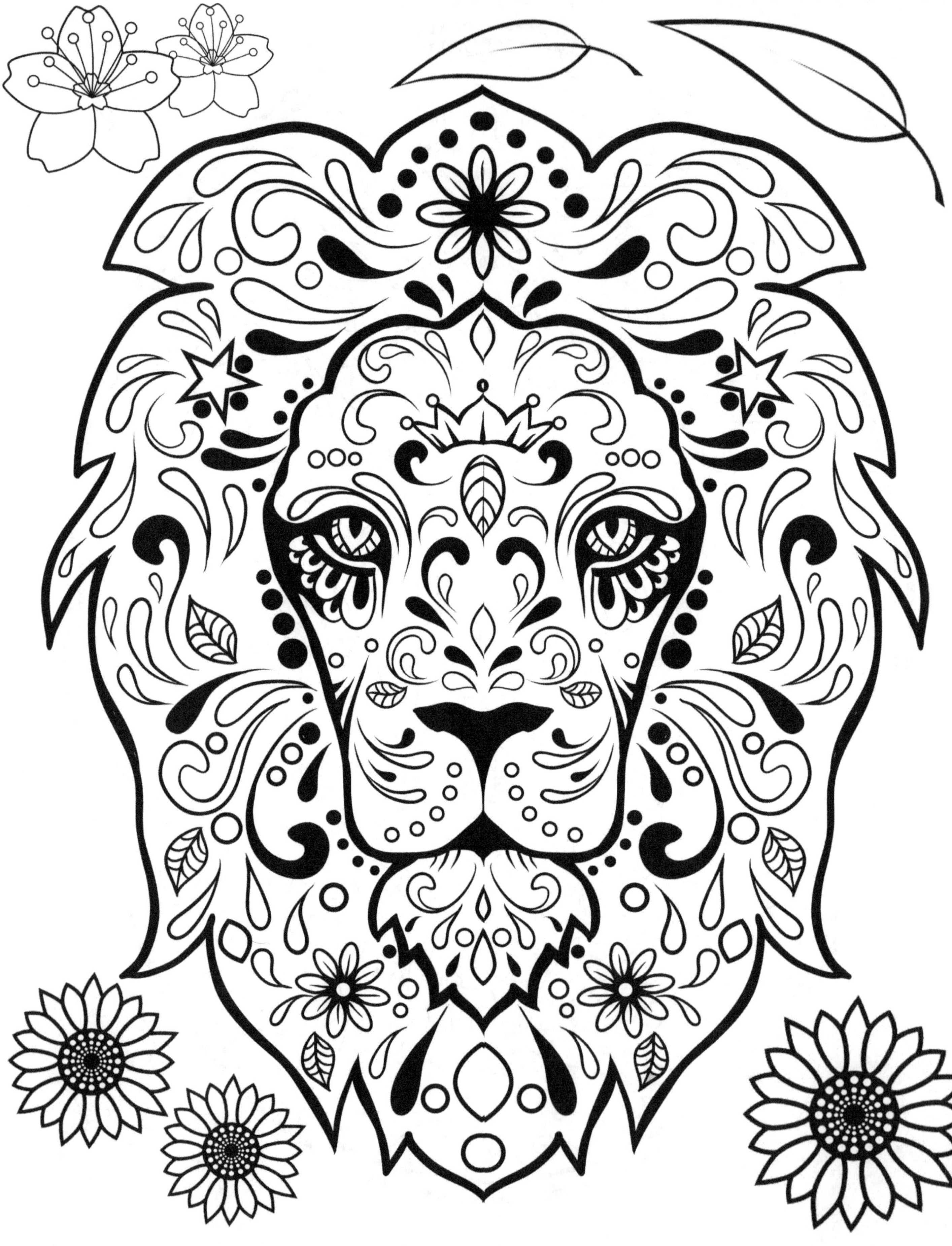

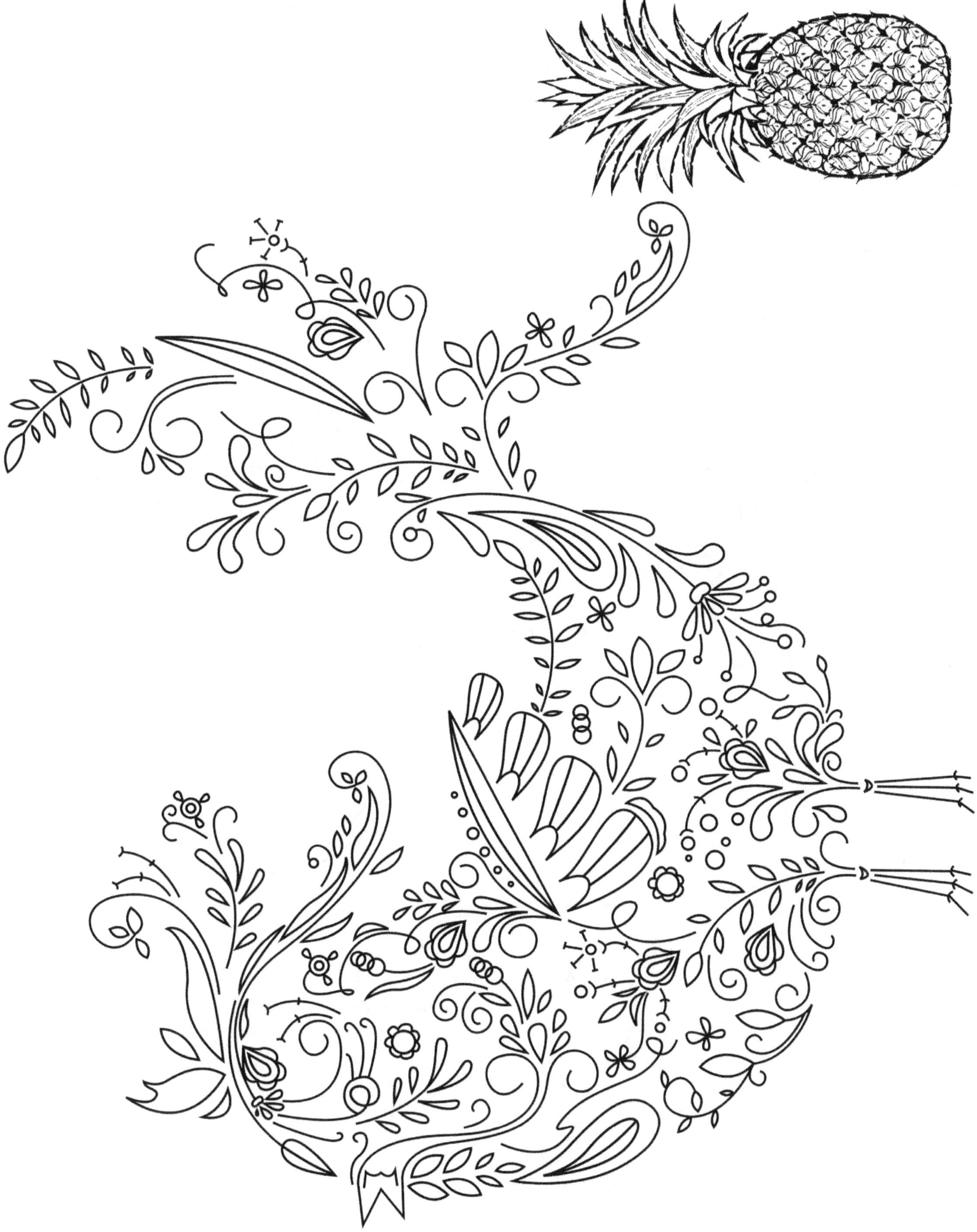

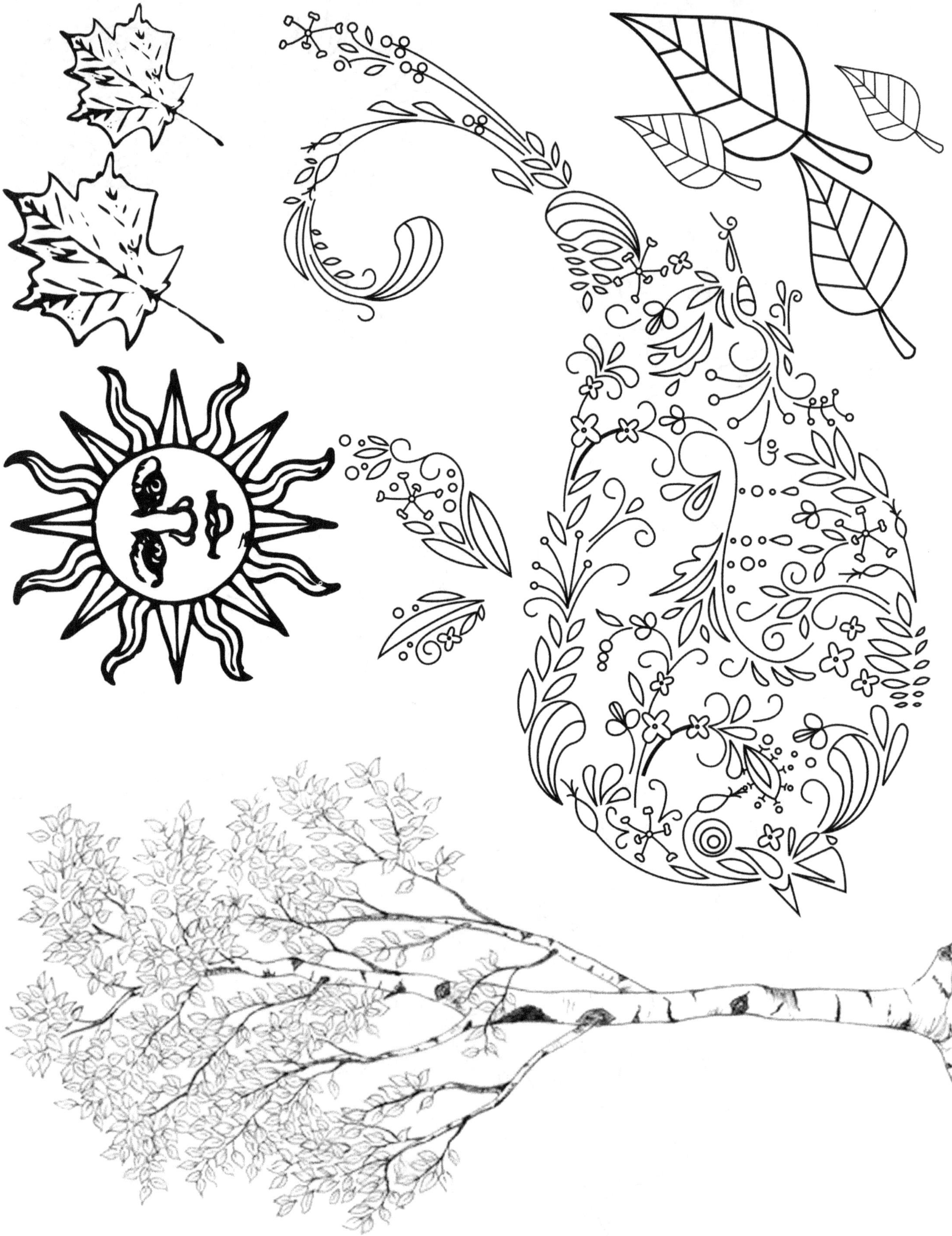

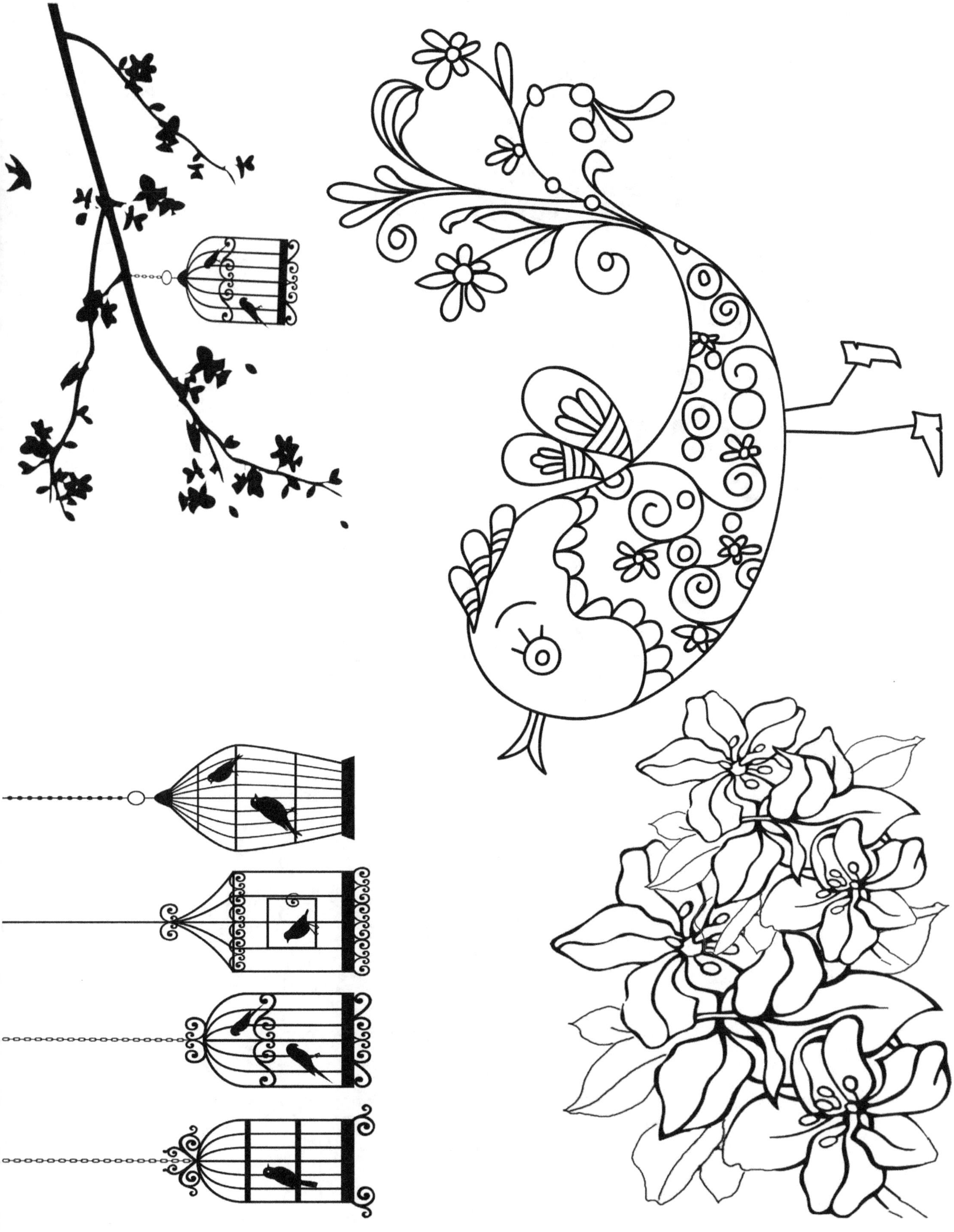

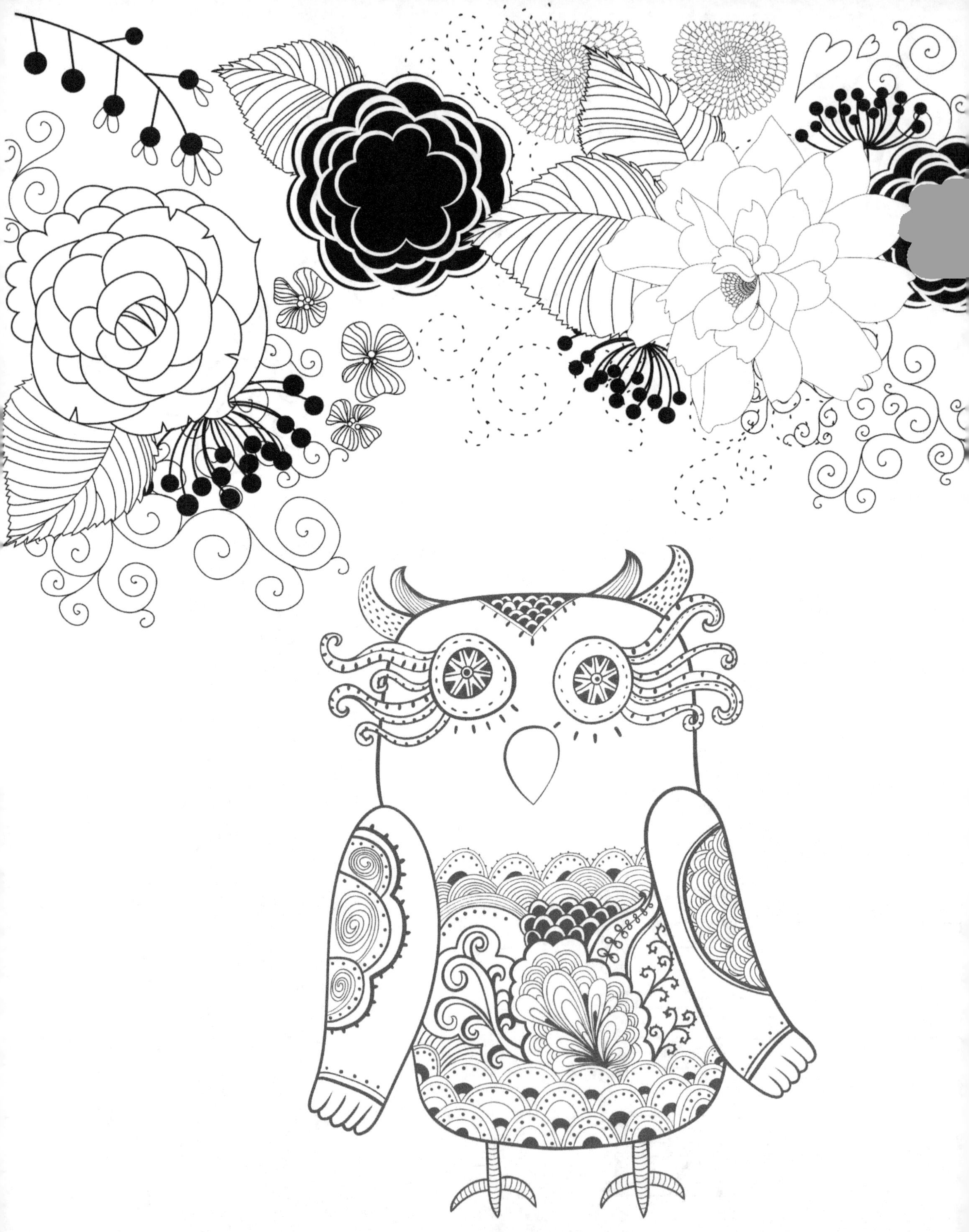

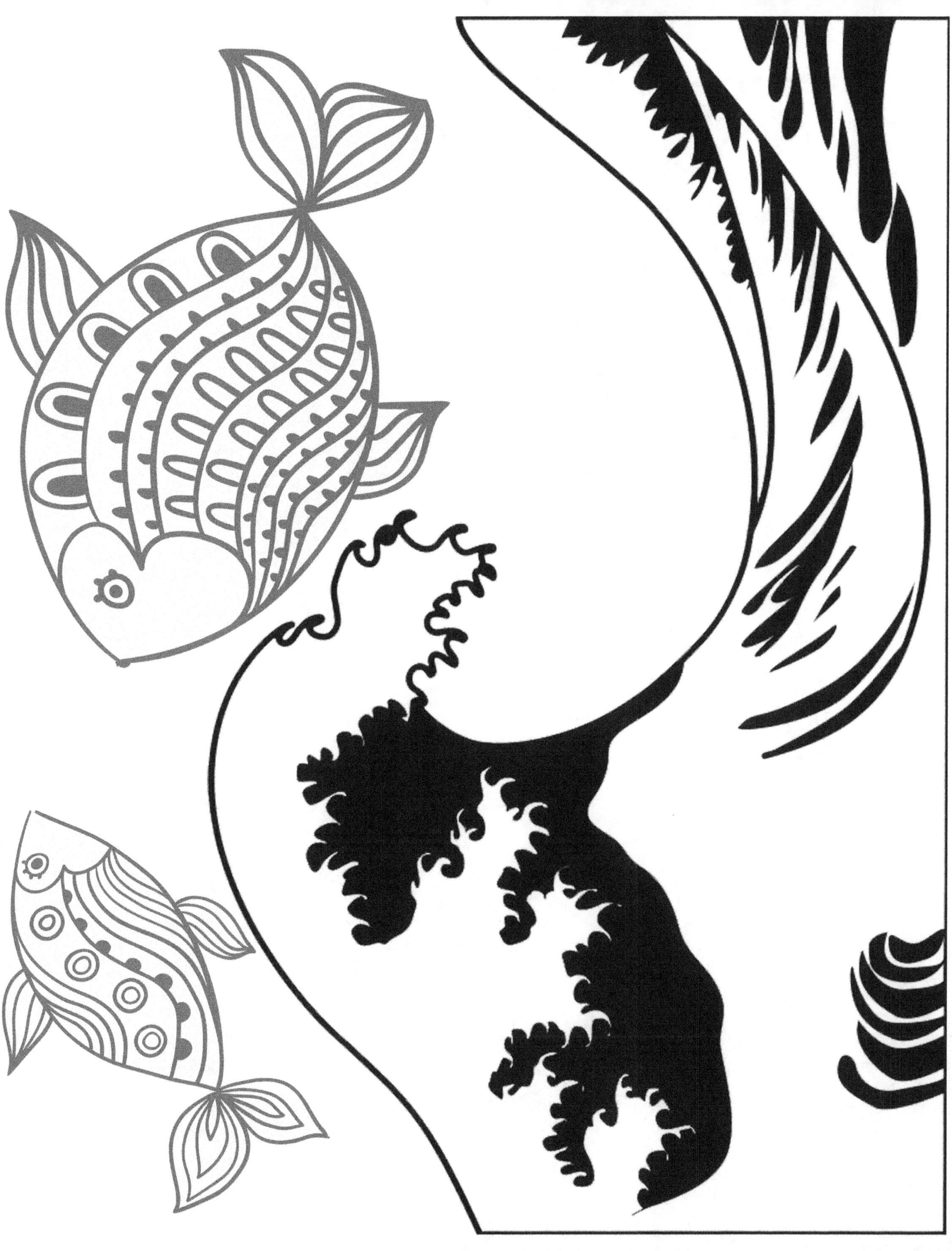

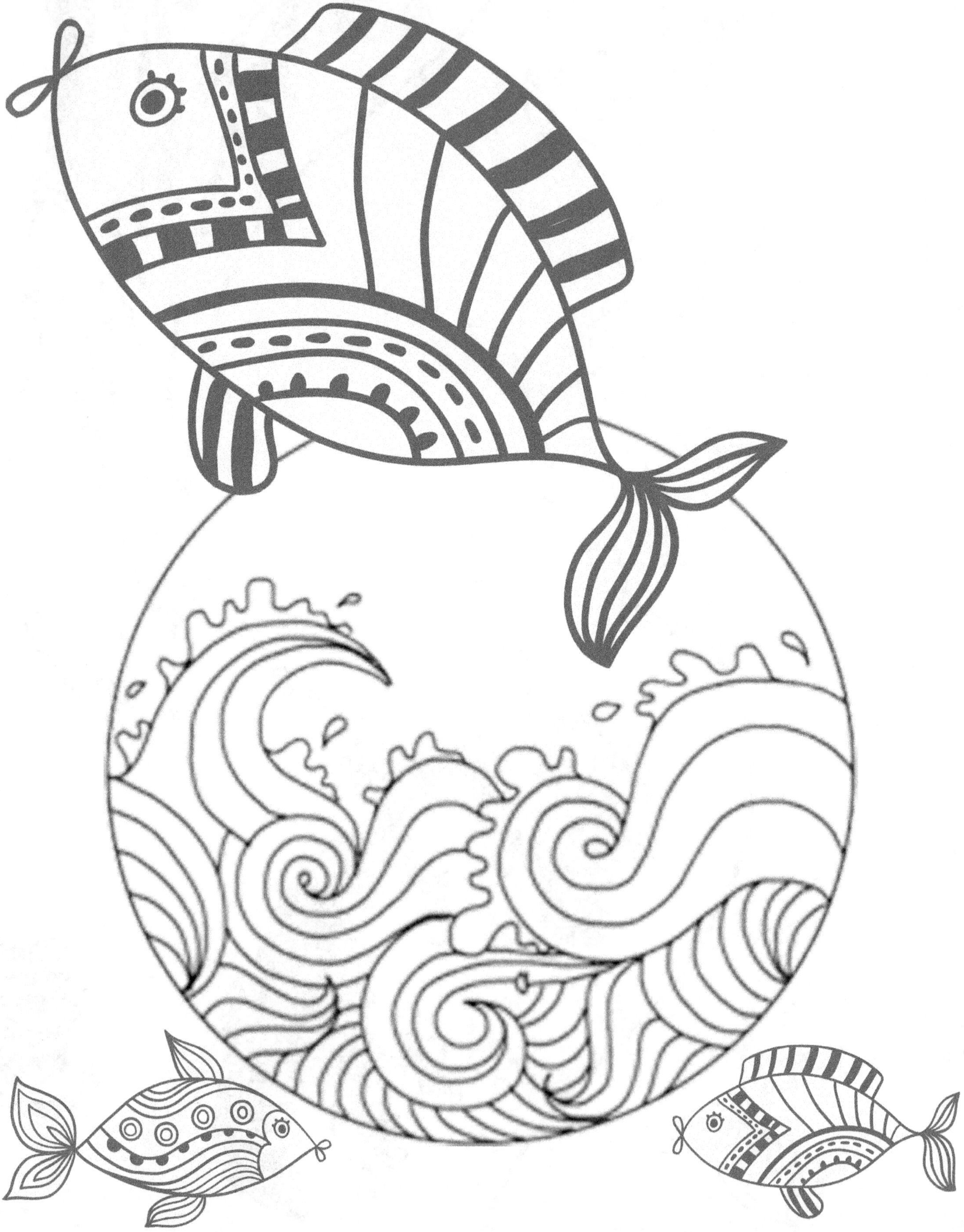

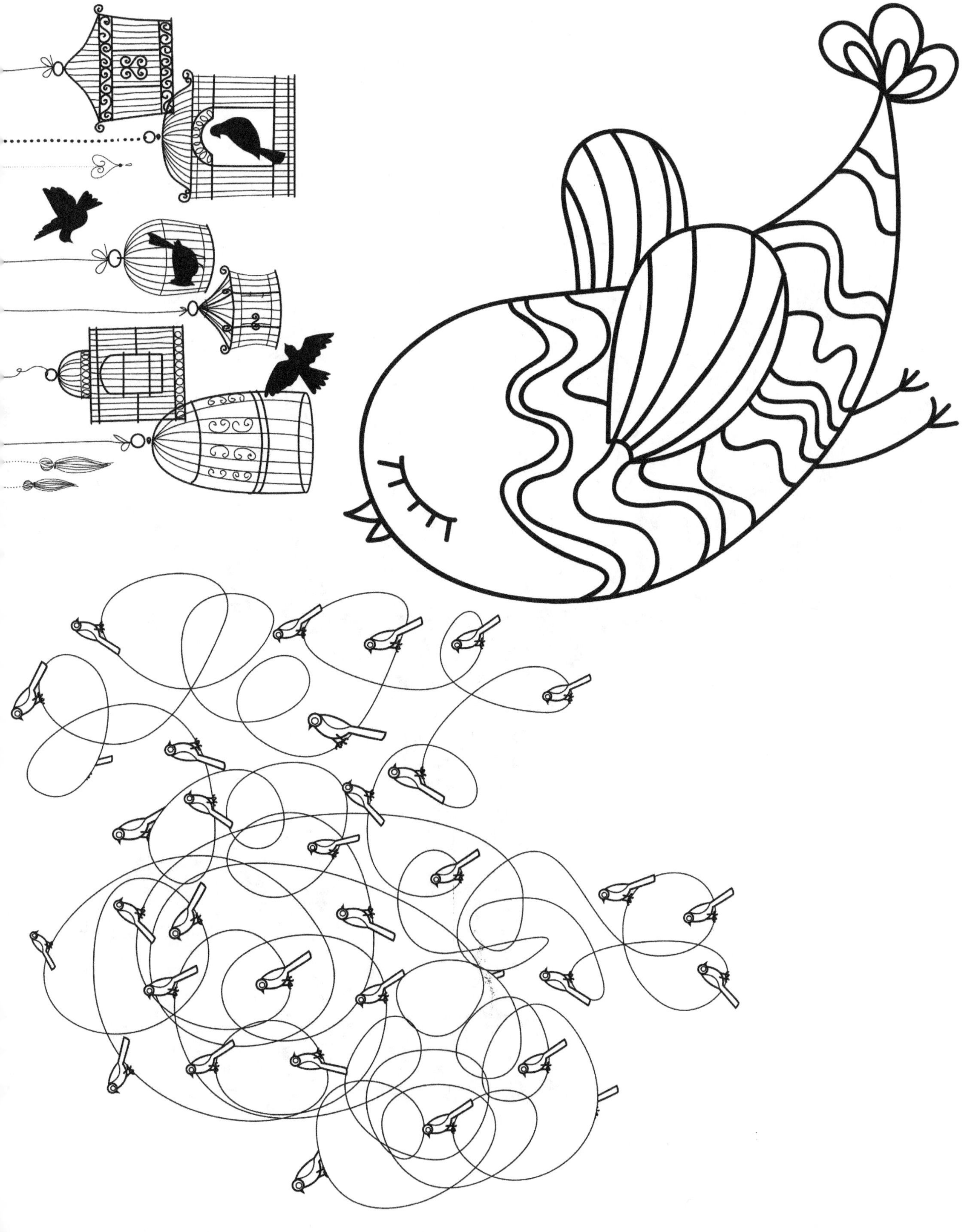

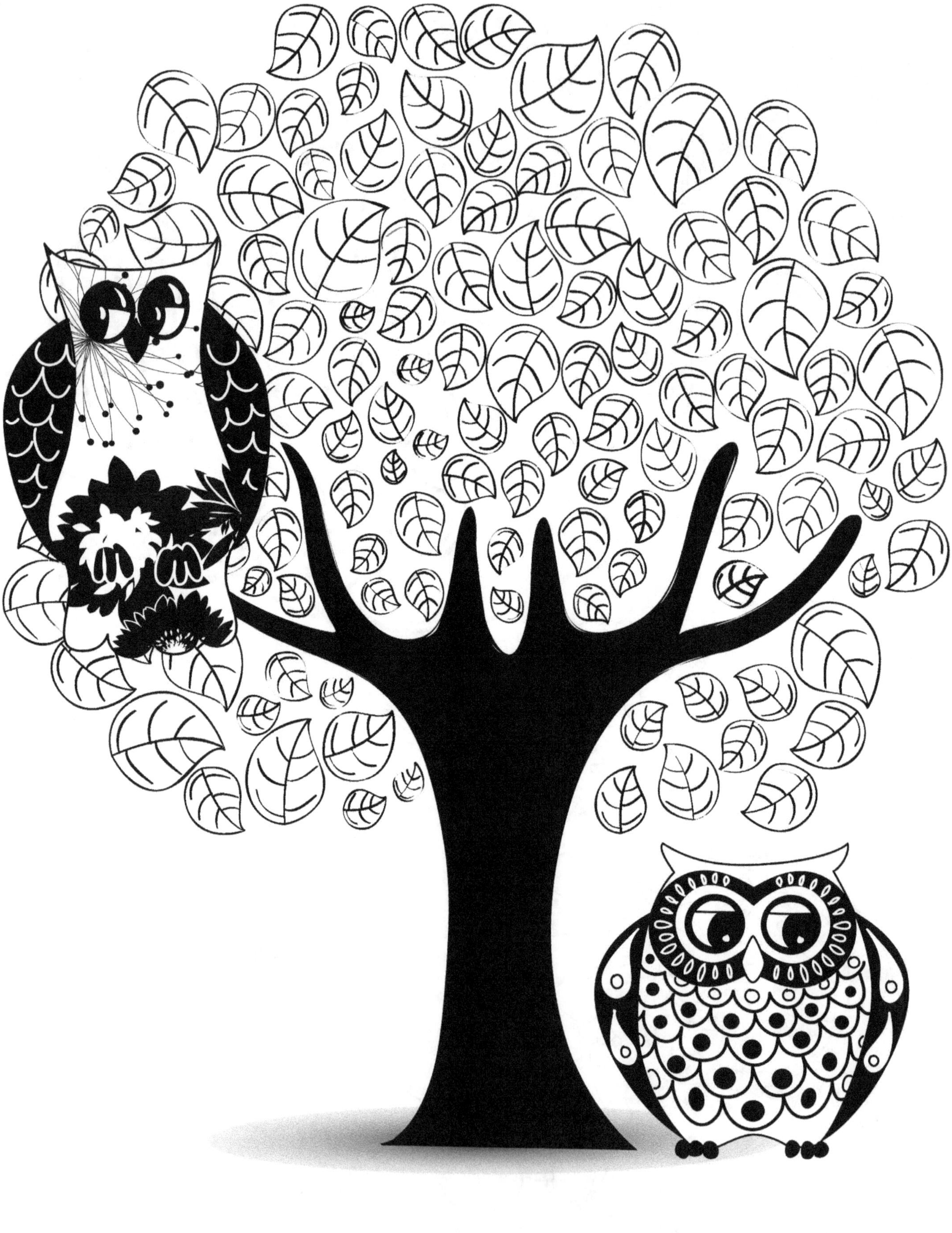

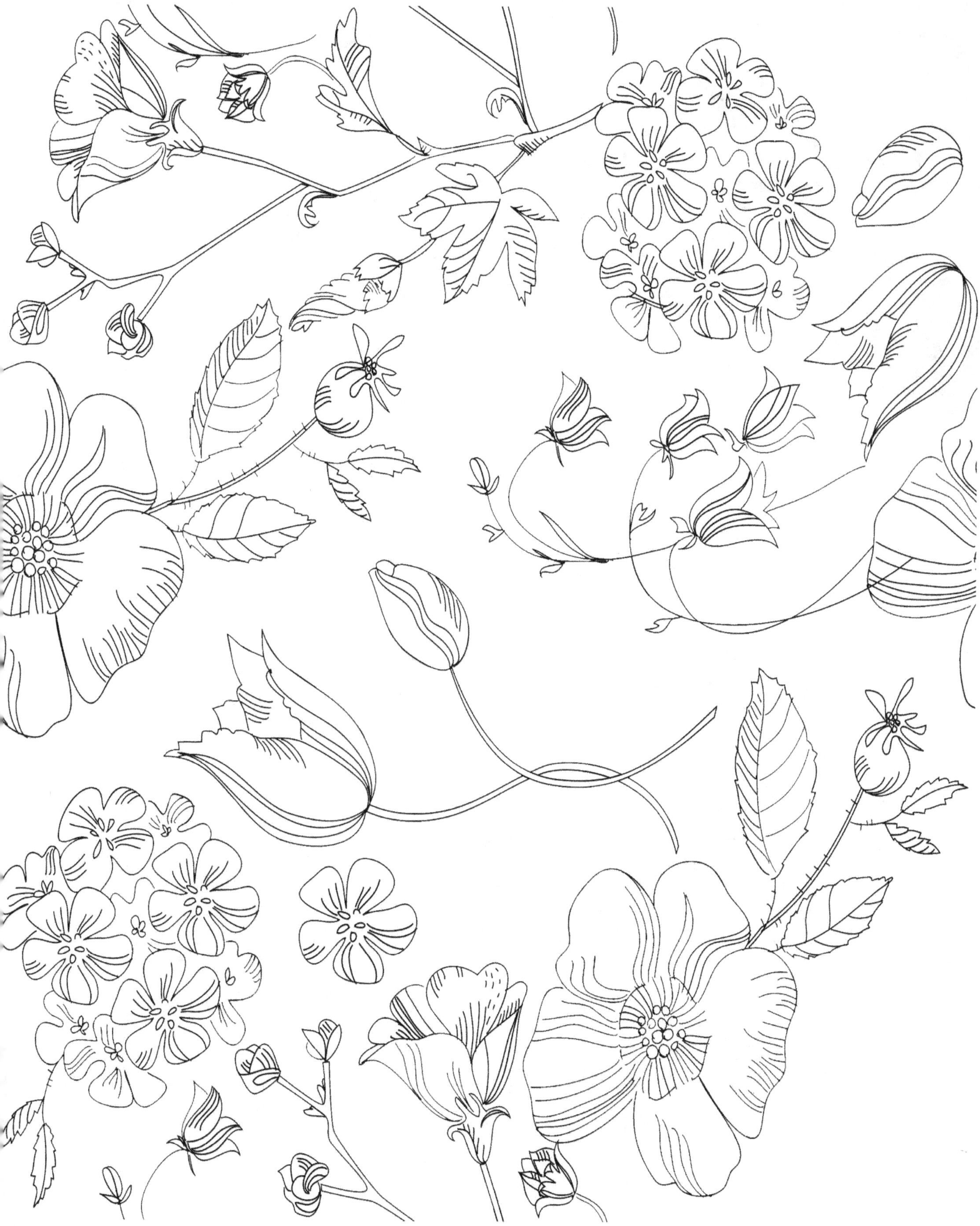

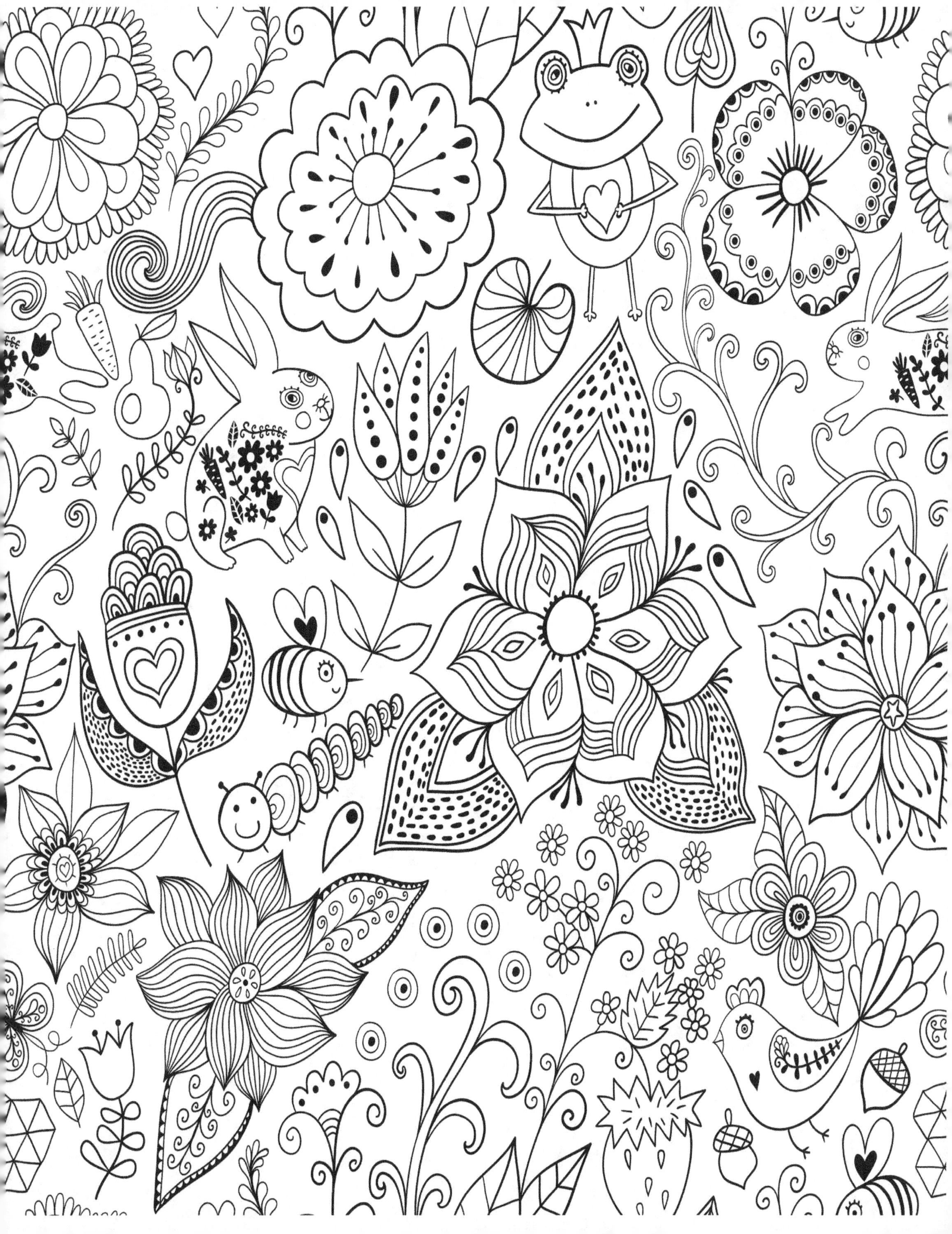

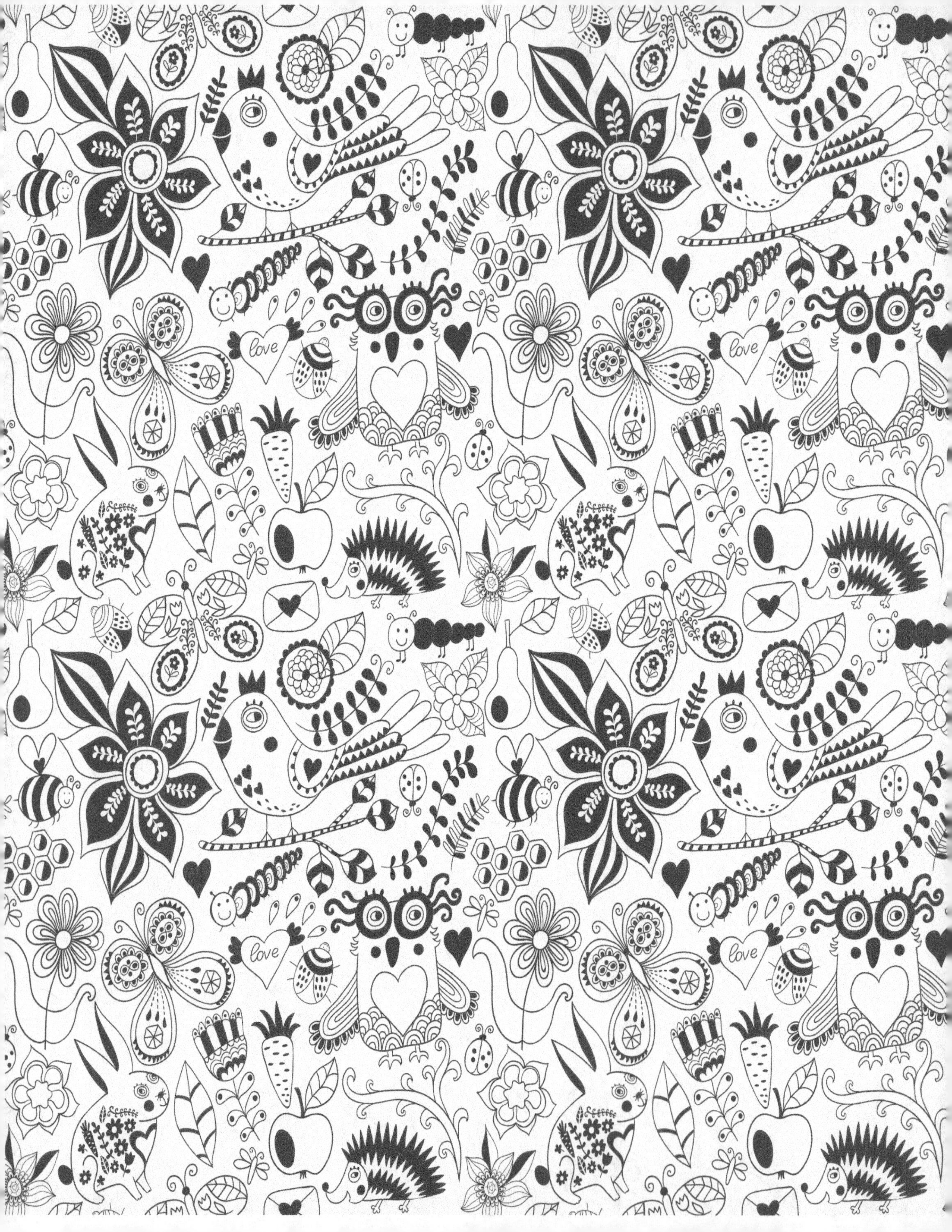
love
love
love
love

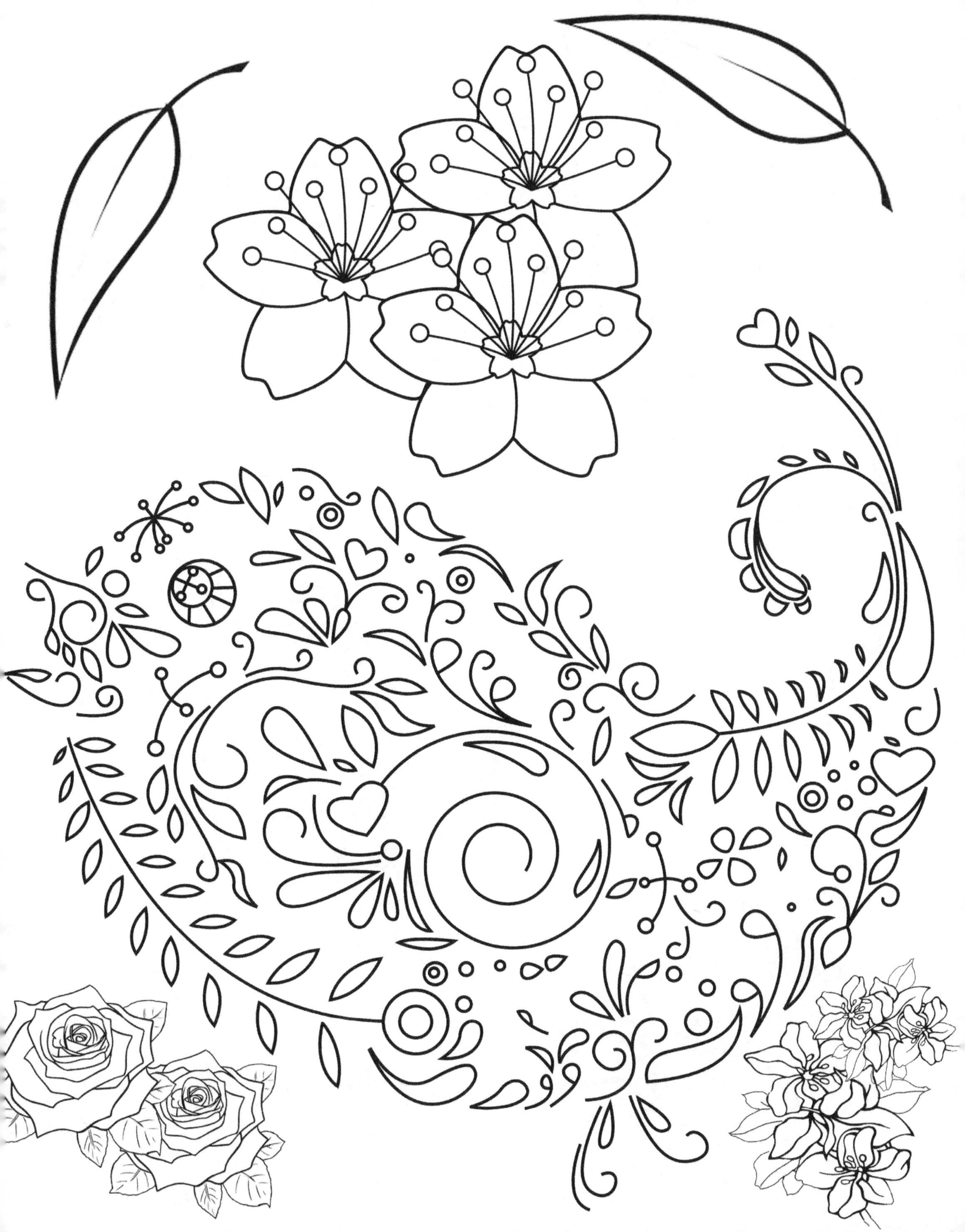

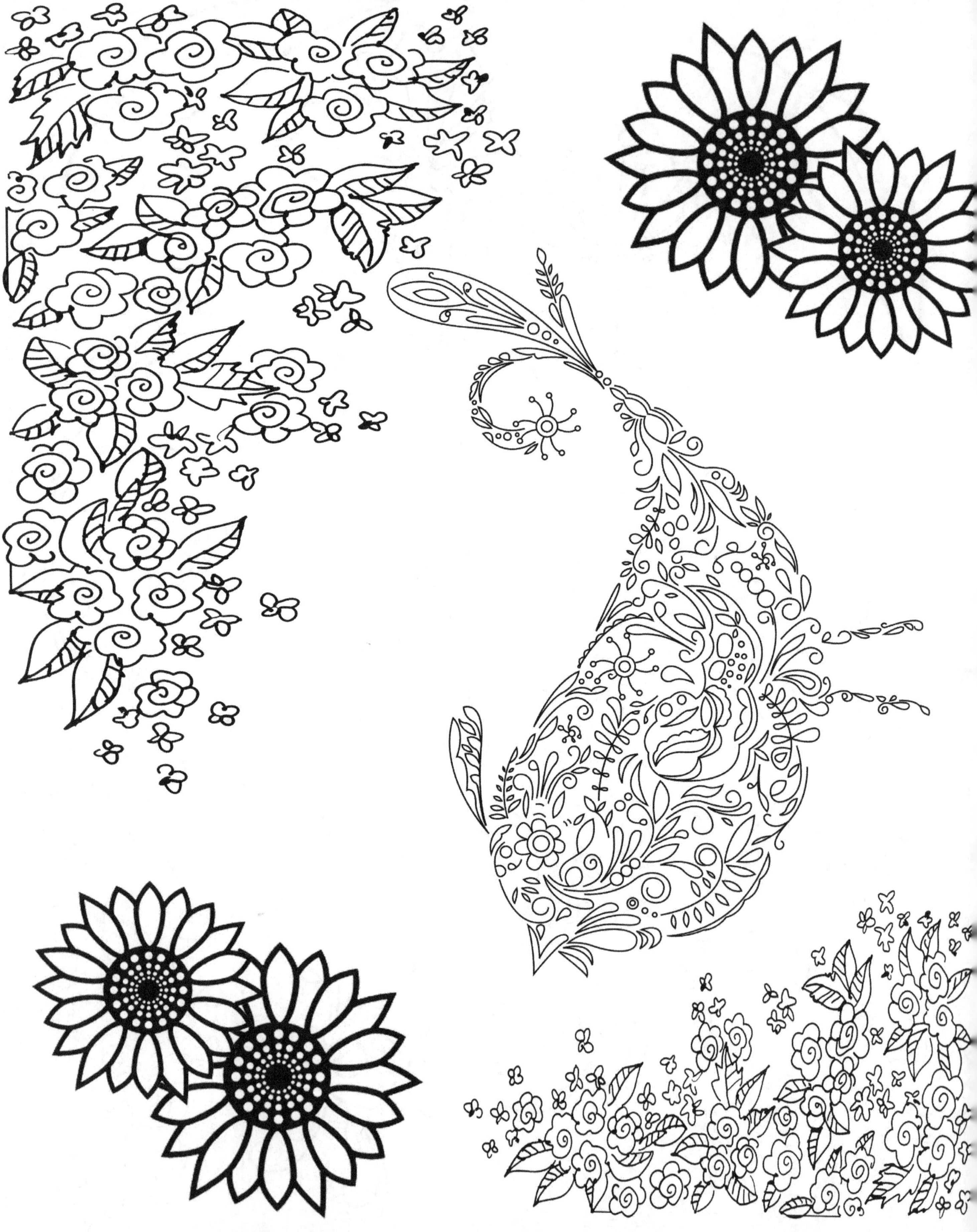

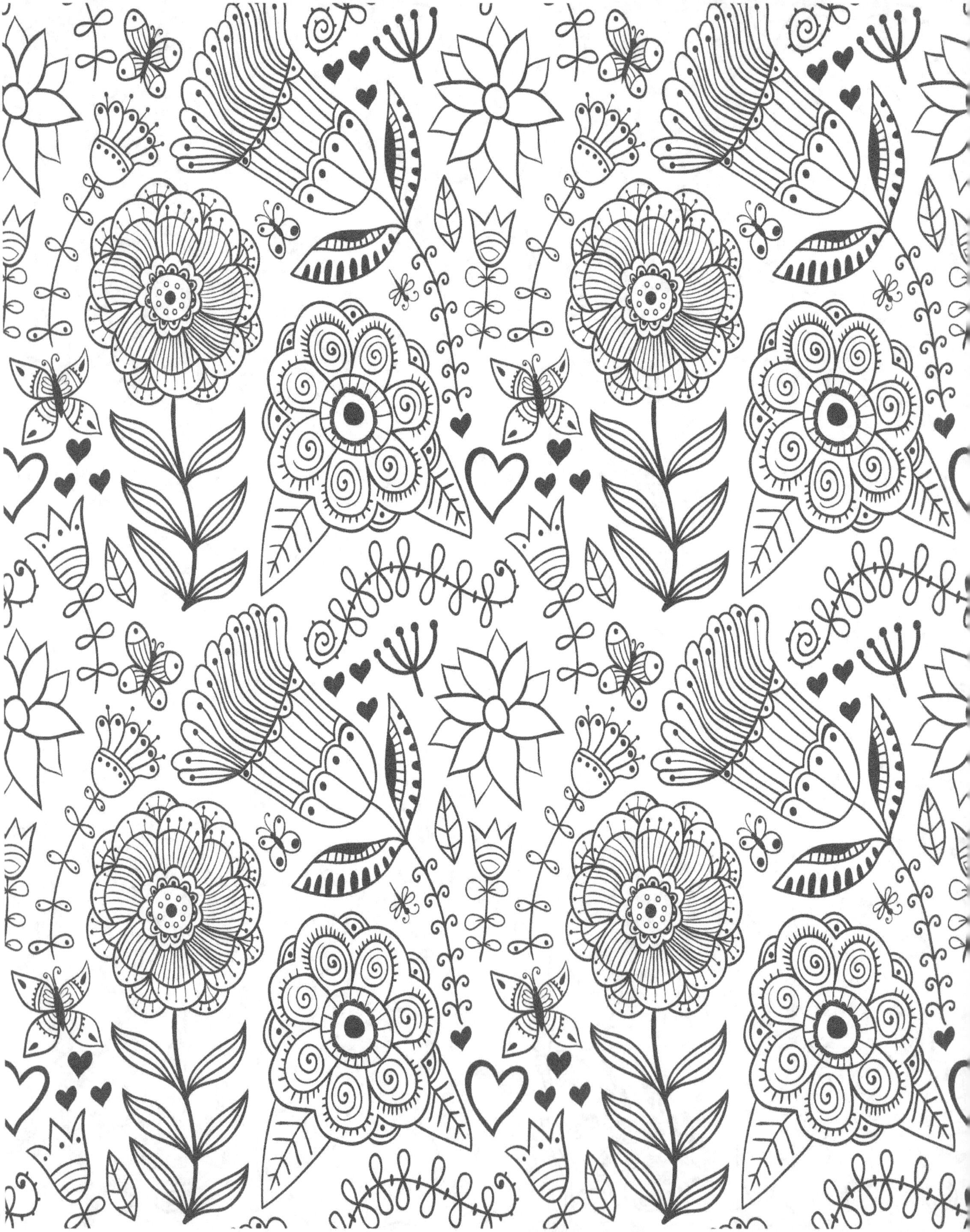

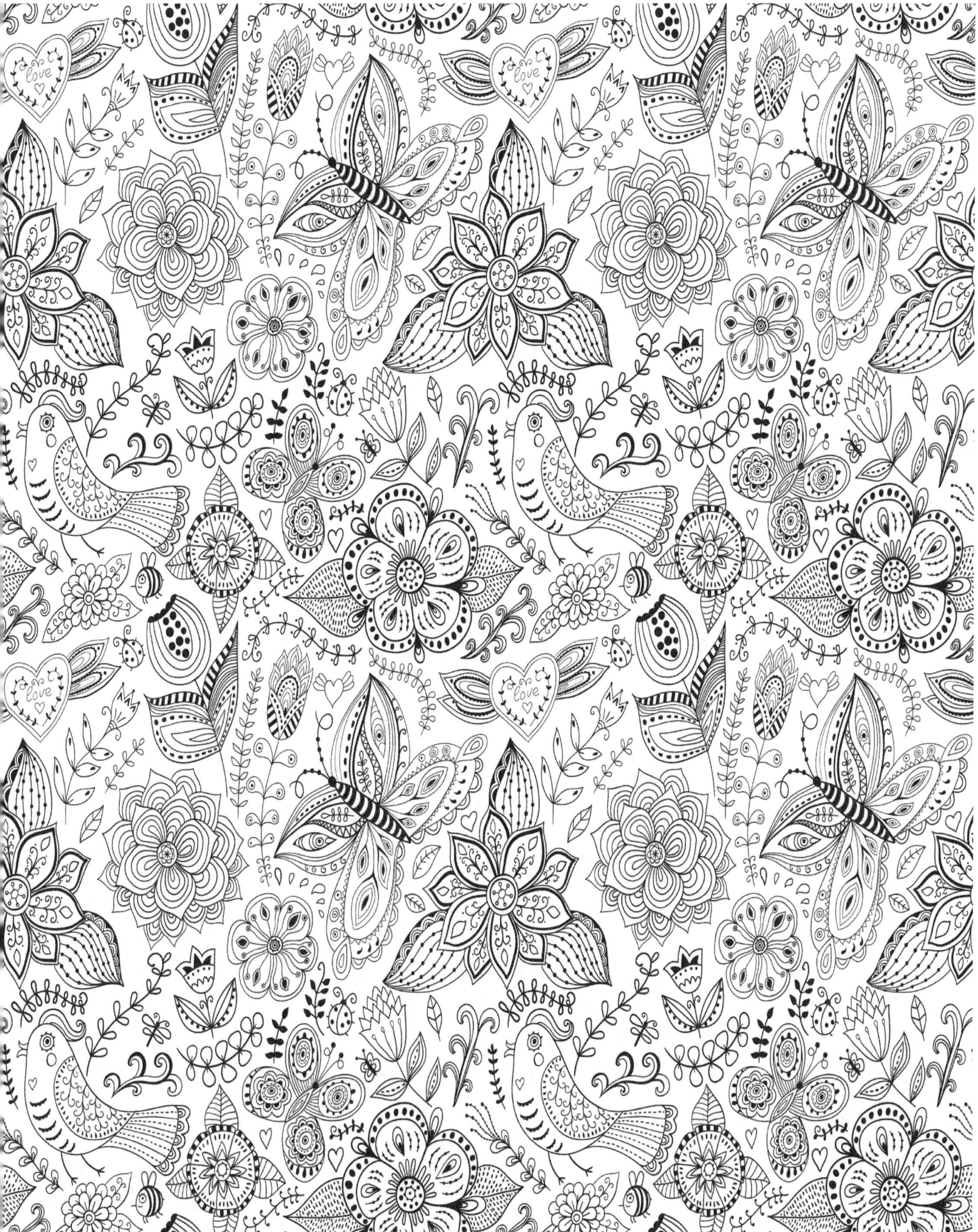
love
love
love
love

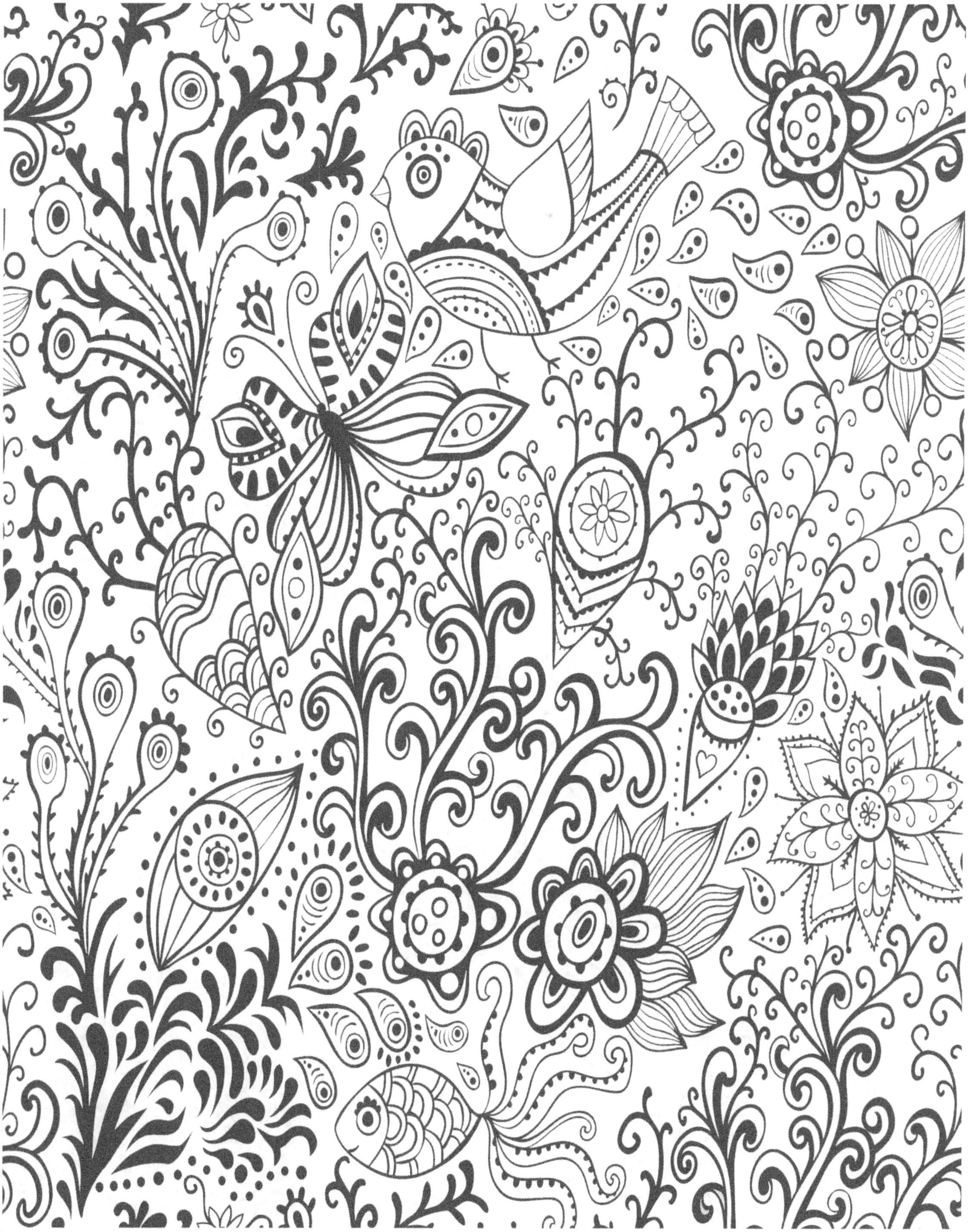

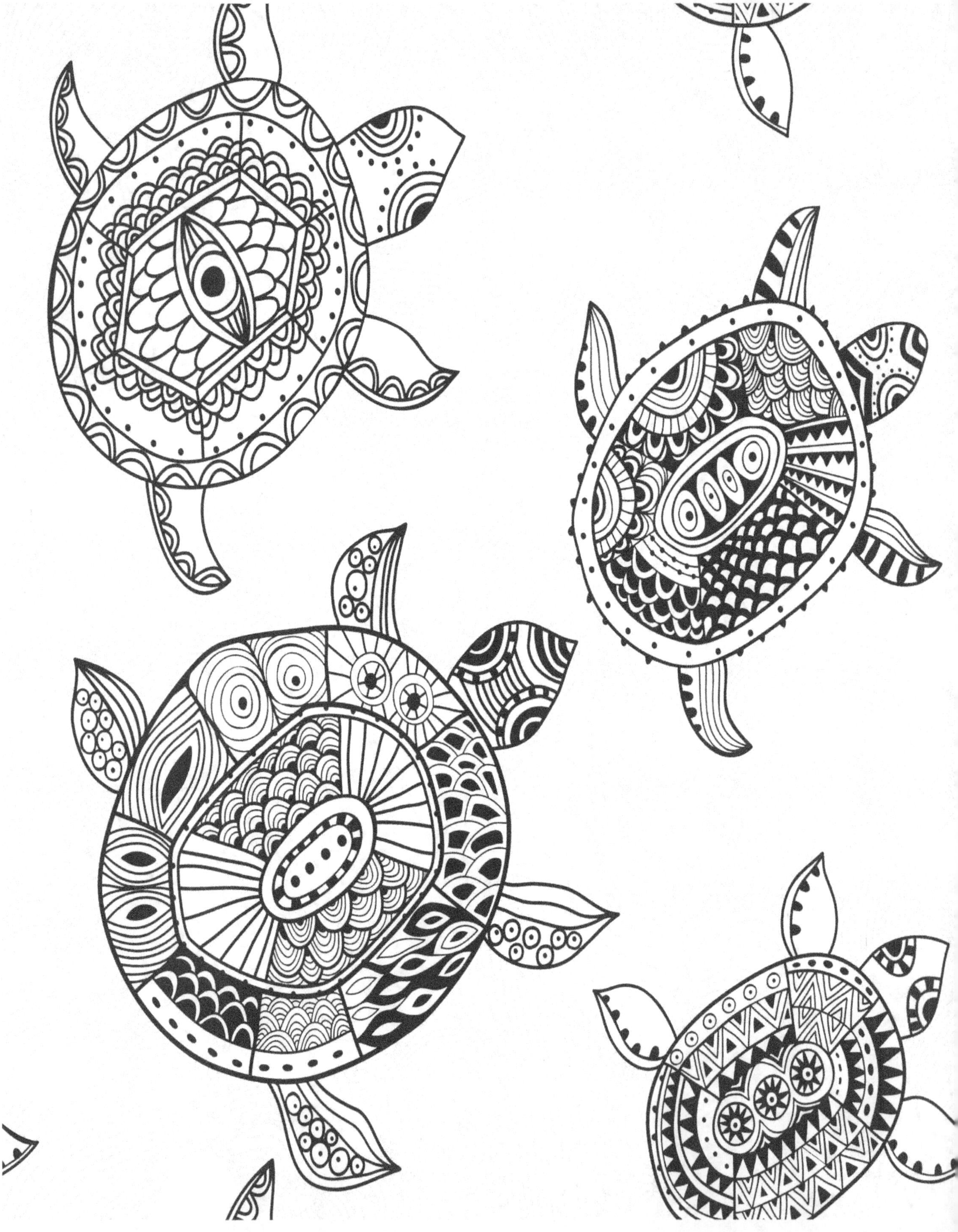

www.ingramcontent.com/pod-product-compliance
Lightning Source LLC
Chambersburg PA
CBHW080645190526
45169CB00009B/3507
9781533213815